Welcome to the launch of . . .

**THE INTERGALACTIC JOKE BOOK.**

To boldly joke, where no man has joked before!

Every space joke under the sun, and a whole lot from even further on. Every one guaranteed to put you into orbit.

You'll be glad you bought this joke book. In fact, you'll be over the moon.

Other joke books
available in Knight Books:

BOBBY DAVRO LAUGH-A-MINUTE
JOKE BOOK
Bobby Davro

THE RIGHT IMPRESSION
Gary Wilmot

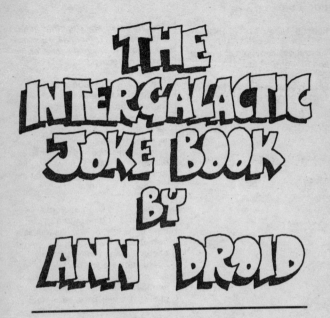

# THE INTERGALACTIC JOKE BOOK BY ANN DROID

Illustrated by
Jeremy Tapscott

**KNIGHT BOOKS**
Hodder and Stoughton

## For Tom

First published in Great Britain in 1989 by Knight Books

Printed and bound in Great Britain for Hodder and Stoughton paperbacks, a division of Hodder and Stoughton Ltd., Mill Road, Dunton Green, Sevenoaks, Kent TN13 2YA (Editorial Office: 47 Bedford Square, London WC18 3DP) by Richard Clay Ltd, Bungay, Suffolk. Photoset by Rowland Phototypesetting Ltd, Bury St Edmunds, Suffolk.

**British Library C.I.P.**

Droid, Ann
  The intergalactic joke book.
  I. Title
  828'.91402

ISBN 0-340-51105-2

# ANDROIDS, ASTEROIDS, ASTRONAUTS, ALIENS AND ATOMIC SCIENTISTS

Who gets congratulated when they're down and out?
*Astronauts.*

Why is an astronaut like a baseball player?
*They both want to make safe touch-downs.*

What do you get if you cross R2-D2 with C3PO?
*Androidful mess.*

What smells good in a spaceship?
*Unidentified frying objects.*

A Martian spaceship landed in an empty petrol station, and the leading Martian went straight up to a petrol pump and said, 'Take me to your leader'. There was no answer. 'Oi, mate,' said the Martian. 'Take your finger out of your ear when I'm talking to you.'

What do you call an Italian astronaut?
*A specimen.* (Say it again with an Italian accent!)

What do astronauts wear to keep warm?
*Apollo-neck jumpers.*

What did the astronaut say to mission control?
*'I'm over the moon.'*

Where are starfish found?
*In a planet-arium.*

Why is astronomy so popular?
*Because it's a heavenly job.*

Why do astronauts wear bullet-proof suits?
*To protect themselves from shooting stars.*

Why did the astronomer hit himself on the head?
*Because he wanted to see stars.*

# BIG BANGS, BLACK HOLES, BLAST-OFFS AND BIONIC BOOSTERS

What's best for mending dents in spaceships?
*Apollo Filla.*

What do you call a mad spaceman's watch?
*A lunar-tick.*

Who's president of outer space?
*Ronald Ray Gun.*

Who's the dumbest person in the Empire?
*Daft Vader.*

What space vehicles skim over the water and
bark at cats?
*Hovercrufts.*

What happened when the cow jumped over the
moon?
*The price of milk rocketed.*

How did the cow jump over the moon?
*She followed the Milky Way.*

What is lighter, the sun or the earth?
*The sun — it rises every morning.*

**Knock, knock.**
  Who's there?
**Saturn.**
  Saturn who?
**Saturnight Fever.**

What do you call a crazy spaceman?
*An astronut.*

How do astronauts play badminton?
*With space shuttles.*

Did you hear about the man who thought a
Rover 2000 was a bionic dog?

# COSMIC CLONES,
# COMETS AND
# COSMONAUTS

How do Martians drink tea?
*Out of flying saucers.*

What's stupid and orbits the moon?
*A loony module.*

Who ran a double-glazing firm in the Empire?
*Draught Evader.*

What did the NASA computer say to the
programmer?
*'You can count on me.'*

What do you get if you cross the sea with a
spaceship computer?
*A brain-wave.*

What is a robot's favourite meal?
*Silicon-chips.*

Why did the robot go mad?
*Because it had a screw loose.*

What did the loony nuclear physicist try to grow in his greenhouse?
*An atomic energy plant.*

What's another name for a space walk?
*A Star Trek.*

Where does Superman buy his breakfast cereal?
*At the supermarket, of course.*

What's black and white and flies around the world?
*Supernun.*

Who is big and hairy and smells?
*Phew-Bacca.*

# DEATH-RAY DOCTORS AND DISEMBODIED DALEKS

What's horrible and floats in space?
*A nasteroid.*

Where does K9 live?
*The dog-star.*

When are soldiers like aliens?
*When they're Martian along.*

Where do astronauts get their pintas?
*From milk craters.*

What do you call a flea that lives in a Martian's ear?
*A space invader.*

What does a baby Martian call its parents?
*Mum and Dad.*

What flies around the earth jabbering on and on about the stars?
*Sputnik Moore.*

How does an astronaut's pet bird land in an emergency?
*By sparrow-chute.*

Who *didn't* invent the very first flying machine?
*The Wrong Brothers.*

What flies around space headquarters and wobbles?
*A jellycopter.*

# EXTRA-TERRESTIALS AND ELECTRONIC EARTHLINGS

What does ET stand for?
*Because he can't sit.*

Why did ET get a shock?
*He received the phone bill.*

What did ET's mother say when he got home?
*Where on Earth have you been?*

What's made of flour and floats in space?
*A pastaroid.*

**1ST ASTRONAUT:** I always have six meals a day when I'm flying in rough weather.
**2ND ASTRONAUT:** Six? How's that?
**1ST ASTRONAUT:** Three down, three up.

How do toads fly in space?
*By hoppercraft.*

When can't astronauts land on the moon?
*When it's full.*

Why are there no dogs on the moon?
*Because there aren't any trees.*

What kind of star wears sunglasses?
*A film star.*

What is the difference between the sun and a loaf of bread?
*One rises from the east and the other from the yeast.*

What did the big star say to the little star?
*You're too young to stay out at night.*

What goes on in a planetarium?
*An all-star show.*

What is the beginning of eternity,
    The end of time and space;
The beginning of every end,
    And the end of every race?

*The letter E.*

# FLYING SAUCERS, FIREBALLS AND FOURTH DIMENSIONOIDS

Two creatures from outer space landed by a traffic light. 'I saw her first,' said one. 'So what?' said the other. 'I'm the one she winked at.'

**MAN:** How does it feel to hurtle through space?
**ASTRONAUT:** It hurtles.

What space film was Dracula in?
*The Vampire Strikes Back.*

Who was R2-D2's father?
*R1-D1.*

Which game is played by spacemen?
*Astro-noughts and crosses.*

What do you get if you cross a spaceship
computer with a boat?
*A row-bot.*

What happened to the robot who ate too much?
*It got atomic-ache.*

Why is a spacecraft like a tramp?
*They both have no visible means of support.*

What does an astronaut do when he gets angry?
*He blasts off.*

What is yellow and wobbly and goes up and
down at over 1,000mph?
*A bowl of custard in a rocket.*

What is the centre of gravity?
*The letter V.*

What do astronauts get if they do their
calculations correctly?
*Gold stars.*

# GALACTIC GRAFFITI, GRAVITY BUSTERS AND GRUESOME GREEN GREMLINS

What do you get if you cross a miserable man with a space-ship?
*A moan-rocket.*

How does a Martian count to twenty-six?
*On his fingers.*

WARNING: Space is the only place graffiti is allowed! Never write graffiti yourself – you need space-ial permission!

Why did Mickey Mouse go on a journey to outer space?
*Because he wanted to find Pluto.*


Why is the letter G like the sun?
*Because they are both the centre of light.*


How many balls of string would it take to reach the moon?
*One, if it was long enough.*


What do you get if you cross a computer with an enormous monster from outer space?
*A two-ton know-all.*

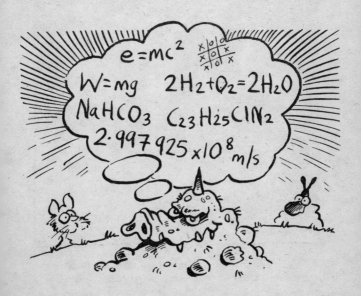

What is more nourishing, a cow or a shooting star?
*A star, because it is meteor (meatier).*

What is the most musical planet?
*Nep-tune.*

# HALLEYS HOWLERS,
# HOVERCRAFT AND
# HEAVENLY HUMANOIDS

Why is Lassie like Halley's comet?
*They're both stars with tails.*

What do you call a space magician?
*A flying saucerer.*

What did the astronaut see in his frying pan?
*An unidentified frying object.*

What do you call a cow in outer space?
*A stargrazer.*

How many letters are there in the alphabet?
*Twenty-four – ET went home.*

What alien has the best hearing?
*The eeriest.*

What step should you take if you have a close encounter with an alien?
*Very large ones – in the opposite direction!*

What did the Martian say when he landed in a flower-bed?
*'Take me to your weeder.'*

What did the spaceman say when he trod on a bar of chocolate?
*'I've just set foot on Mars.'*

What is the best way to talk to a Martian?
*By long distance.*

What is the easiest way to see flying saucers?
*Trip up a waiter.*

# INTERGALACTIC INVADERS AND IONOSPHERIC IDIOTS

Where do Daleks buy their food?
*Dalekatessens*.

What did the sign on the astronaut's door say?
*GONE TO LAUNCH*.

What do computers eat?
*Fission chips*.

Two birds were sitting on a tree not far from
Cape Canaveral. Suddenly a spaceship roared
through the sky close by them. 'Cor, look at that!'
said one. 'What's so surprising?' said the other
one. 'I bet you'd go fast if your tail was on fire!'

What car do robots drive?
*A Volts-wagon.*

Why did the robot grease his joints before going to bed?
*Because he wanted to get up oily in the morning.*

What do you call a musical robot that eats too much?
*Heavy Metal.*

Who was the first animal in space?
*The cow that jumped over the moon.*

Why can't elephants fly in space?
*Because their trunks won't fit under the seat.*

What astronaut is always in a hurry?
*A Russian.*

What astronaut wears the biggest space helmet?
*The one with the biggest head.*

How many ears has Captain Kirk got?
*Three – the left ear, the right ear, and the final frontier.*

# JUMPING JUPITER JOKES

**MARTIAN TO HIS FRIEND:** What's that revolting ugly thing on your neck? Oh sorry, it's your head!

What dish is out of this world?
*A flying saucer.*

Do robots have brothers?
No, *only transistors.*

**1ST ASTRONAUT:** Can you telephone from a spaceship?
**2ND ASTRONAUT:** Of course I can tell a phone from a spaceship!

When is the moon heaviest?
*When it's full.*

Name a shooting star.
*Clint Eastwood.*

**Knock, knock.**
    Who's there?
**Mars.**
    Mars who?
**Marsock's got a hole in it.**

How did Mary's little lamb get to the moon?
*By rocket sheep.*

**Knock, knock.**
  Who's there?
**Jupiter.**
  Jupiter who?
**Jupiter go home now.**

Why are aliens forgetful?
*Because everything goes in one ear and out the others.*

What is soft, white and sweet and comes from Mars?
*Martian mallows.*

# KRAZY KRYPTONOIDS AND KAHOUTEK KNOCK KNOCKS

Who cleans Hans Solo's boots?
*Shoeblacker.*

Which is more important, the sun or the moon?
*The moon. It shines when it's dark, but the sun shines when it's light anyway.*

What do you eat somewhere over the rainbow?
*A way-up pie.*

What game do spacemen play?
*Moonopoly.*

Two astronauts arrived at the Pearly Gates. St Peter said, 'If you'll just wait a moment I'll check your files and see if I can let you in.' 'Actually, we don't want to come in,' said one of the astronauts. 'Really?' said St Peter. 'Then exactly what *do* you want?' 'Please sir,' said the second astronaut, 'can we have our satellite back?'

What turned the moon pale?
*Atmos-fear.*

How do you phone the sun?
*Use a sun-dial.*

Which is the noisiest planet?
*Saturn, because it has so many rings.*

Why are false teeth like stars?
*Because they come out at night.*

What's yellow and blue with a twenty-metre wing span?
*A two tonne budgie.*

What's the best thing to say when a Martian aims his laser gun at you?
*'I give up.'*

Where does a Martian with a laser-gun sleep?
*Anywhere he wants to.*

What did the space policemen say to the three-headed alien?
*'Hello, hello, hello.'*

# LASERS, LIGHT-YEARS AND LUNAR LUNACY

Martin Martian was travelling by himself in his spaceship. As he hovered over a farm, he called down to the farmer: 'Hallo, Earthling. Where am I?' The farmer looked up. 'You can't fool me,' he shouted. 'You're up there in that little spaceship!'

What do you call a Martian pub?
*A Mars bar.*

What do you get if you cross an astronaut's gun with a cheer and a hippopotamus?
A *hip-hippo-ray-gun*.

'*Doctor, doctor, I keep seeing green Martians in front of my eyes.*'
'Have you seen a psychiatrist?'
'*No, just green Martians.*'

How do you get a baby astronaut to sleep?
*You rock-et.*

What did the astronaut say about the ten-legged aliens?
'*Don't worry, they're armless.*'

# BOOKS FROM THE LUNAR LIBRARY

* *Astrology* by Horace Cope
* *Blast-Off* by Count Down
* *Looking Through My Telescope* by I. C. Stars

* *Nuclear Energy* by Molly Cule
* *Space Communications* by Moss Code
* *Space Power* by Alec Tricity
* *Too Near the Sun* by Eamonn Fire
* *Walking on the Moon* by Betty Fawls
* *Back From My Space Travels* by Jeff A.
  Nicetime
* *The Thing From Outer Space* by A. Lee-En
* *Talking to Mars* by Roger N. Dowt
* *Equipped for Space Travel* by Kit Ed Outrite

# METEORS, MARTIANS AND MAN-IN-THE-MOON MADNESS

Why wasn't the pub that the astronaut opened on the Moon a success?
*It had no atmosphere.*

What do you get if you cross a round black hat with a rocket?
*A very fast bowler.*

How does a robot sit?
*Bolt upright.*

What do you get if you cross the Moon with the top of a house?
*A lun-attic.*

What was the scientist's reaction when he discovered electricity?
*He was shocked.*

Who is a space scientist's favourite movie actor?
*Robot de Niro.*

Who was the first man in space?
*The man in the moon.*

**1ST ASTRONAUT:** What happens if we're up in space and we run out of fuel?
**2ND ASTRONAUT:** We get out and push.

What should an astronaut never do?
*Look down.*

What is an astronaut's favourite snack?
*A Mars bar.*

What do you get if you cross a skunk with an astronaut?
*An animal that stinks to high heaven.*

What does Luke Skywalker shave with?
*A laser blade.*

What do you call wobbly invaders?
*Return of the Jelly.*

# NEPTUNES, NUCLEAR NEWS AND NEUTRON NONSENSE

What do you get if you cross a group of stars with a silver cup?
*A constellation prize.*

**SPACE TEACHER:** If we breathe oxygen in the daytime, what do we breathe at night?
**SPACE PUPIL:** Nitrogen?

What is a flying saucer?
*A dish that is out of this world.*

What is fission?
*An atomic scientist's favourite sport.*

**Knock, knock.**
  Who's there?
**Doctor.**
  Doctor who?
**That's right.**

What did one Invisible Man say to another?
*'It's nice not to see you again.'*

What did the space alien say to his girlfriend?
*'I wanna hold your hand, hand, hand, hand . . .'*

What did the traffic light say to the Martian?
*'Don't look now, I'm changing.'*

What's small and brown and travels at 100mph?
*ET on a motorbike.*

How does an alien impress people?
*It puts its beast foot forward.*

What did the Martian say when he landed on Brighton beach?
*'Take me to your Lido.'*

What's yellow and round and hovers over the kitchen?
*An unidentified frying omelette.*

# ORBITAL OBJECTS AND OUTER SPACE ODDITIES

What happens when Martians hold a beauty contest?
*Nobody wins.*

'Waiter, waiter, there's a strange film on my soup.'
*'What do you expect for 40p – Star Wars?'*

What is written on a Dalek's tombstone?
*Rust in peace.*

**BOY:** Dad, what's nuclear fission?

**FATHER:** Er, I'm afraid I don't know anything about atomic energy.

**BOY:** Well, how does a space ship land on the moon if there's no gravity there?

**FATHER:** Sorry, son, I don't really know much about space travel either.

**BOY:** Oh. Can you tell me how jets assist a vertical take-off, then?

**FATHER:** Mmm, you've got me there, I'm afraid.

**BOY:** You don't mind me asking you all these questions, do you Dad?

**FATHER:** Of course not, son. You have to ask questions if you want to learn anything . . .

What do you call an astronaut who's afraid of heights?
*A failure.*

Sign seen at Mission Control during blast-off:
WATCH THIS SPACE.

What illness do astronauts suffer from?
*Flu!*

Why did the Invisible Man look in the mirror?
*To see if he still wasn't there.*

The first two men in space were really dumb.
One set out on a space walk, leaving the other
in charge of the spacecraft. After a while, the
one inside heard a knock at the door. 'Who's
there?' he asked.

# PLUTONIUM PULSARS AND PLANETARY PUNS

Why did the mad atomic scientist take a ruler to bed?
*To see how long he slept.*

Which Martians have their eyes nearest together?
*The smallest Martians.*

What do you get if you swallow uranium?
*Atomic ache.*

Why did the germ from Venus cross the microscope?
*To get to the other slide.*

**SPACE TEACHER:** What does $HNO_3$ stand for?
**SPACE PUPIL:** $HNO_3$? Let me think . . . It's on the tip of my tongue . . .
**SPACE TEACHER:** Well spit it out at once! It's nitric acid!

Where do robots fight?
*In a scrapyard.*

What goes 'Mooz . . .'?
*An upside-down rocket.*

Why doesn't the sea fall into space?
*Because it's tide (tied).*

What do you get if you cross a rocket with a kangaroo?
*A space shuttle that makes short hops.*

What is an astronaut's favourite meal?
*Launch.*

What did the astronaut say as he kissed his wife good-bye?
*'Must fly now . . .'*

What does an astronaut do when he's dirty?
*He has a meteor shower.*

What do you call a space prison?
*A sput-nick.*

# QUASAR QUIPS

**SPACE TEACHER:** What is an atom?
**SPACE PUPIL:** The man who lived in the Garden of Eden with Eve.

**SPACE TEACHER:** This space is deadly poisonous. What steps would you take if it escaped?
**SPACE PUPIL:** Jolly big ones!

Knock, knock.
  Who's there?
Soup.
  Soup who?
Souperman.

**SPACE TEACHER:** Light travels from the Moon towards Earth at the rate of 299,000 kilometres per second. Don't you think that's remarkable?
**SPACE PUPIL:** Not really. It's downhill all the way.

What is a cow's favourite TV programme?
*Dr Moo.*

A Martian space traveller returns to Mars after a trip to the planet Earth. 'What do you think of this suit?' he asks his commander, 'I had it made in Hong Kong.' 'Very nice,' replied the commander. 'But what's that hump on the back?' 'Oh that's the tailor,' said the Martian. 'He's still working on it.'

**SPACE TEACHER:** Name a liquid that cannot freeze in space.
**SPACE PUPIL:** Boiling water.

Why did Darth Vader turn down streaky bacon at the butcher's?
*Because the Empire likes back.*

What is more invisible than the Invisible Man?
*His shadow.*

Where do spacemen park their rockets?
*At parking meteors.*

What is woolly, covered in chocolate, and goes round the sun?
*A Mars baa.*

# ROCKETS, ROBOTS AND RADIOACTIVE RIBTICKLERS

What would you do if you met a blue Martian?
*Try to cheer him up.*

What is long and yellow and travels great distances?
*An intercontinental banana missile.*

What stars go to prison?
*Shooting stars.*

What are space fleas called?
*Lunar-tics.*

BOING!

What do Mars, the Galaxy and the Milky Way
have in common?
*They're all chocolate bars.*

What do you call an asteroid that thinks it's
being followed?
*A paranoid.*

What do astronauts suffer from if they sit down
too long?
*Asteroids.*

What is an astronomer?
*A night watchman with a good education.*

What does the Invisible Man call his mum and
dad?
*His transparents.*

What do you call a flying space policeman?
A *helicopper*.

What do you call a space insect?
An *astro-gnat*.

What is pie in the sky?
A *flying pizza*.

# SPACE SCHOOL, SPACE SHUTTLES, SUPERMEN AND SUPERSONIC SILLINESS

Two drunks were staggering home one night. One looked up at the sky and said, 'Is that the sun or the moon?' 'I don't know,' replied the other. 'I don't live around this area.'

**ASTRONAUT TO WIFE:** Did you miss me when I was gone?
**WIFE:** Were you gone?

Did you hear about the man who stayed up all night trying to work out what happened to the sun when it went down?
*It finally dawned on him.*

What did one space computer say to another space computer?
*'I've got lots of problems . . .'*

What did the robot say to his girlfriend?
*'I love you watts and watts . . .'*

What is a kangaroo's favourite TV programme?
*Dr Roo.*

What do you get if you cross a planet with a toad?
*Star Warts.*

Why is a prisoner like an astronaut?
*They're both keen on outer space.*

What do you call an alien who talks through his nose?
*An adenoid.*

What is the difference between the rising sun and the setting sun?
*A day.*

Where does K9 go for his holidays?
*Pluto.*

Did you hear about the astronauts' football match?
*The winners were over the moon.*

# TITANS, TRITONS AND TIME TRAVELLERS

Why did the robot act silly?
*Because he had a screw loose.*

'How was the new science fiction film you saw?'
*'Oh, you know – same old story: boy meets girl, boy loses girl, boy builds new girl . . .'*

What did the robot say to his girlfriend?
*'You're so electrocute.'*

What is bacon's favourite tune?
*Fry Me To The Moon.*

What was Batman doing in the sky?
*Aerobatics.*

Did you hear about the space computer that
worked so hard it broke down?
*The doctor diagnosed metal fatigue.*

**Knock, knock.**
  Who's there?
**Dan Dare.**
  Dan Dare who?
**Dan Dare in de great big hole.**

What is the Invisible Man's favourite drink?
*Evaporated milk.*

72

A very spoilt child was annoying other passengers by lying in the aisle of the space shuttle. One particularly irritated man turned to the child and said, 'Hey kid, why don't you go and play outside?'

What is better than presence of mind when a Martian aims his laser gun at you?
*Absence of body.*

What do you get if you cross Darth Vader with a cricket referee?
*The Umpire Strikes Back.*

What's green and flies around the world?
*Super-pickle.*

# UNIVERSES, UNHUMANOIDS AND UNBELIEVABLE UFOS

**MRS MARTIAN:** Why do they call your son Wonder Boy?
**MRS VULCAN:** Because people look at him and wonder.

What did one shooting star say to the other?
*'Pleased to meteor.'*

What do astronauts play football on?
*Astro-turf.*

Heard on a shuttle a million kilometres out in space: 'Ladies and gentlemen, this is your captain speaking. I have some good news and some bad news. The good news is that we have perfect visibility, clear weather, and we are making record time. The bad news is, we're lost!'

**PASSENGER ON SHUTTLE:** Look at all those people down there. They look just like ants.
**HOSTESS:** They are ants – we haven't taken off yet.

What do you call a beetle from space?
*Bug Rogers.*

If an athlete gets athlete's foot, what does an astronaut get?
*Missile-toe.*

What's purple and floats in outer space?
*The Planet of the Grapes.*

What happens when the cow that jumped over the moon meets Taurus the bull?
*Steer Wars.*

Did you hear about the astronaut who planned to fly to the sun?
*He knew it was hot, so he decided to go at night.*

What goes up and never comes down?
*Your age.*

**NERVOUS ASTRONAUT TO GROUND CONTROL:** Do spacecraft crash often?
**GROUND CONTROL:** Only once.

What do you get if you cross a germ with a potato?
*A microbe-chip.*

# VENUS, VELOCITY AND VULCAN VULGARITIES

**FAT VULCAN:** They say that travel broadens one.
**SKINNY EARTHLING:** My goodness, you must have been around the universe.

If a being was born on Earth, raised on the Moon, came to Venus, and died on Mars, what is he?
*Dead.*

**MAN AT SPACE SHUTTLE TERMINAL:** We just flew in from the moon.
**OTHER MAN:** I bet your arms are tired.

What did the mother robot say to the little robot when he came home after midnight?
*'Wire you insulate?'*

What kind of jokes did Einstein make?
*Wise-cracks.*

What creatures swim in space?
*Starfish.*

What is the dog star?
*Lassie.*

What has twenty-two legs and two wings but
can't fly?
*The astronauts' football team.*

Why did the Invisible Man go mad?
*Out of sight, out of mind.*

What is long and green, has one bionic eye, and
fights crime?
*The Six Million Dollar Cucumber.*

What do you call a one-eyed alien on a motor
bike?
*Cycle-ops.*

What happened when the bionic baby was born?
*Nothing – the doctor was too afraid to smack it.*

# WARP FACTORS AND WEIGHTLESS WAITERS

What illness do Vulcans catch?
*Chicken spocks.*

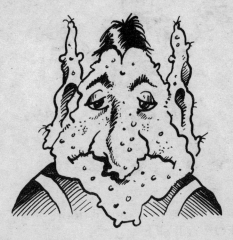

What has pointed ears and eats lettuce?
*Mr Spock on a diet.*

What has three eyes like a Martian, an arm like a Martian, four hands like a Martian, but isn't a Martian?
*A photograph of a Martian.*

Who is a space scientist's favourite poet?
*Robot Burns.*

Which space machine was inspired by a spider to go on and save Scotland?
*Robot the Bruce.*

Sign seen on Mission Control door:
GONE FOR A BYTE.

What did the robot say when it ran out of electricity?
*AC come, AC go.*

How do you arrange a trip to Mars?
*Plan-et.*

What holds the moon up?
*Moon-beams.*

When does an astronaut have his midday meal?
*At launch time.*

# X-RAYS AND X-RATED JOKES

What is the difference between a sleeping
Vulcan and one that is awake?
*With some Vulcans it's hard to tell!*

Did you hear about the alien with five legs?
*His trousers fit him like a glove.*

What do you call an underground train full of atomic scientists?
*A tube of Smarties.*

**SHUTTLE PILOT TO CONTROL:** This is Lunar flight 220 requesting permission to land.
**CONTROL TOWER:** Please state your height and position.
**SHUTTLE PILOT:** 1.7 metres and I'm sitting in the cockpit.

What's red and runs in slow motion?
*The bionic nose.*

'Penelope has just got engaged to an X-ray technician.'
*'I wonder what he sees in her?'*

What's stupid and goes into space?
*A loony module.*

When is a window like a star?
*When it's a sky-light.*

What do you call a fat ET?
*An extra-cholesterol.*

What kind of ears do spaceships have?
*Engin-eers.*

In what year was ET born?
*19 ET 3 (1983).*

# YARNS FROM THE PLANET 'Y'

What's yellow and white and travels at Mach 7?
*A Shuttle pilot's egg sandwich.*

What kind of person watches the stars?
*A cinema-goer.*

What's big, bright and silly?
*A fool moon.*

What's the best thing to do with a green Martian?
*Wait until he's ripe.*

What's green and slimy and goes up and down?
*A Martian in a lift.*

Did you hear about the spaceship that was so old it had an outside toilet?

If the men at Cape Canaveral are so clever, how come they count backwards?

Why does Superman have big shoes?
*Because of his amazing feats . . .*

# INTER-GALACTIC ZOOS AND ZOMBIES

What's brown, round, and travels at 1,000mph?
*An intercontinental ballistic rissole.*

What did the launch pad say to the rocket?
*'Clear off – you're fired!'*

What's green and slimy and has eight wheels?
*A Martian on roller-skates.*

'My budgie died of 'flu.'
    'But budgies don't get 'flu.'
'Mine flew into a space shuttle.'


What's green and slimy with red spots?
*A Martian with measles.*

What would you get if Batman and Robin were trampled on by a herd of stampeding space monsters?
*The Mashed Crusaders.*


What does Spiderman do when he's angry?
*He goes up the wall.*


Did you hear about the bionic man who was caught speeding on the motorway?
*He was fined £200 and dismantled for six months.*

What does Mr Spock eat for breakfast?
*Star Brek.*

Three men were auditioning for a part in Star
Trek. The first man had pointed ears, so he
wanted to play Mr Spock. The second man had
a Scottish accent, so he wanted to play Scottie.
The third man was dressed as a tree. 'What part
do you want?' asked the puzzled producer. 'The
Captain's log,' he replied.

'Doctor, doctor, I keep feeling like the Invisible
Man.'
*'Who said that?'*

# THE RIGHT IMPRESSION

## GARY WILMOT

The Duchess of York, Jimmy Cricket, Mrs Thatcher *and* Madonna in your living room? They could be if you follow Gary Wilmot's advice and make – THE RIGHT IMPRESSION!

Mimic *your* way to success with Britain's brightest star!

**KNIGHT BOOKS**

Education